D0845662

FARM ANIMALS

Turkeys

by Hollie Endres

BELLWETHER MEDIA • MINNEAPOLIS, MN

BLASTOFF! READERS
1

Note to Librarians, Teachers, and Parents:

Blastoff! Readers are carefully developed by literacy experts and combine standards-based content with developmentally-appropriate text.

Level 1 provides the most support through repetition of high-frequency words, light text, predictable sentence patterns, and strong visual support.

Level 2 offers early readers a bit more challenge through varied simple sentences, increased text load, and less repetition of high frequency words.

Level 3 advances early-fluent readers toward fluency through increased text and concept load, less reliance on visuals, longer sentences, and more literary language.

Level 4 builds reading stamina by providing more text per page, increased use of punctuation, greater variation in sentence patterns, and increasingly challenging vocabulary.

Level 5 encourages children to move from "learning to read" to "reading to learn" by providing even more text, varied writing styles, and less familiar topics.

Whichever book is right for your reader, Blastoff! Readers are the perfect books to build confidence and encourage a love of reading that will last a lifetime!

This edition first published in 2008 by Bellwether Media.

No part of this publication may be reproduced in whole or in part without written permission of the publisher. For information regarding permission, write to Bellwether Media Inc., Attention: Permissions Department, Post Office Box 1C, Minnetonka, MN 55345-9998.

Library of Congress Cataloging-in-Publication Data
Endres, Hollie J.
  Turkeys / by Hollie J. Endres.
    p. cm. – (Blastoff! readers. Farm Animals)
Summary: "A basic introduction to turkeys and how they live on the farm. Simple text and full color photographs. Developed by literacy experts for students in kindergarten through third grade"—Provided by publisher.
  Includes bibliographical references and index.
  ISBN-13: 978-1-60014-086-0 (hardcover : alk. paper)
  ISBN-10: 1-60014-086-6 (hardcover : alk. paper)
  1. Turkeys—Juvenile literature. I. Title.

SF507.E47 2008
636.5'92—dc22   2007007466

Contents

Turkeys are birds.
Some turkeys live
in the **wild**.
Some live on farms.

Turkeys have wings.
Most farm turkeys
cannot fly.
Their bodies are
too heavy to fly.

Turkeys have
feathers.
A male turkey
can puff up
its feathers
and **fan** its tail.

9

Turkeys have
a flap of skin
called a **wattle**
on their neck.

wattle

Turkeys have a hard, sharp beak. It helps them pick up small foods such as **grains**.

beak

Turkeys also **graze** on fresh plants.

15

Turkeys are **social**. They stay together in the farmyard.

They **crowd** around the farmer who brings food.

This farmer
takes care of
a lot of turkeys!

Glossary

crowd—to gather closely around someone or something

fan—to spread out

grains—the seeds of plants such as wheat, corn, and oats

graze—to eat living plants

social—living and staying together with others in a group

wattle—a piece of loose skin that hangs from the throat of a turkey

wild—living in nature

To Learn More

AT THE LIBRARY

Bell, Rachael. *Turkeys*. Portsmouth, N.H.: Heinemann, 2003.

Schuh, Mari C. *Turkeys on the Farm*. Mankato, Minn.: Capstone Press, 2002.

ON THE WEB

Learning more about farm animals is as easy as 1, 2, 3.

1. Go to www.factsurfer.com

2. Enter "farm animals" into search box.

3. Click the "Surf" button and you will see a list of related web sites.

With factsurfer.com, finding more information is just a click away.

Index

The photographs in this book are reproduced through the courtesy of: Phillip Holland, front cover; Arco/H. Reinhard, p. 5; robynrg, p. 7; Jeff Banke, p. 9; Stephen Bonk, p. 11; Super Stock, p. 13; Tim Graham/Alamy, pp. 15, 17; Mike Brinson/Getty Images, p. 19; Super Stock, p. 21.